Original title:
The Sapling Saga

Copyright © 2025 Creative Arts Management OÜ
All rights reserved.

Author: Isabella Rosemont
ISBN HARDBACK: 978-1-80566-684-4
ISBN PAPERBACK: 978-1-80566-969-2

Beneath the Canopy

A squirrel danced with glee,
Poking fun at me.
'You call that growth?'
Ha! I'm six feet tall, don't you know?

The sun said, "Let's play,"
While shadows made a ballet.
Leafy hats quite fancy,
In a world that's far too chancy.

Roots tangled in a jest,
Asked the wind for a rest.
"Blow my hair, it's fine!"
Yet they twisted like a vine.

Beneath the shade I thrive,
With laughter, I arrive.
A party in full bloom,
Join us, don't be doomed!

From Seed to Splendor

I started small and shy,
Like a sprout saying goodbye.
Yet dreamed of skies so wide,
And a trunk to take in stride.

The worms gave me a nudge,
Said, "Grow big—don't budge!"
Now I'm high and proud,
Perched above a chatting crowd.

The sun, my loyal friend,
Winks at me till the end.
"Keep reaching for the light!"
I'll grow taller, what a sight.

A bird perched on my head,
Said, "You're a cozy bed!"
Life's funny little turns,
In my branches, laughter burns.

A Leafy Odyssey

Once a seed, I took a ride,
On the breeze, I felt the glide.
Next to trees and buzzing bees,
I learned to dance with leafy ease.

A bug popped on my leaf,
Claimed, "I'm the king, no grief!"
I rolled my eyes, oh dear,
Do bugs even have a beer?

Raindrops fell like jokes from high,
Tickling me as they passed by.
"I'm the splashy sort," I said,
"Let's make puddles instead!"

With every breeze, I smiled wide,
For together, we abide.
Nature's laughter through the trees,
In my branches and the breeze.

Evergreen Aspirations

In a world of green attire,
I reached for stars like fire.
'Plant a dream,' said the breeze,
'And grow tall with so much ease.'

The pitchforks and the spades,
Joined the dance with leafy shades.
One said, "Watch for those knaves!"
As we jived with garden graves.

The rain poured jokes like wine,
Each drop a punchline, so divine.
I twirled beneath the clouds,
A giggling root, oh so proud.

Turning seasons can't deter,
A leafy life, that's my spur!
Together let's make hay,
In the fun of every day!

A Canopy of Possibilities

Underneath the leafy shade,
A squirrel plotting his parade.
With acorns stacked up high and neat,
He dreams of snacks and tasty treats.

The branches sway, a dance so grand,
A tiny bird leads the band.
With chirps and tweets, they sing a tune,
While blossoms twirl, a lovely boon.

The sun peeks through, like a game of hide,
A tickle on the bark, in joy we glide.
As shadows play tag, we laugh aloud,
In this green realm, we're all so proud.

A breeze arrives, a funny sight,
Ruffled leaves take off in flight.
The laughter echoes through the boughs,
In nature's fun, we take our vows.

Roots in the Whispering Wind

Beneath the ground, the roots conspire,
They giggle low, as they aspire.
To tickle bugs and tease the soil,
In their secret world, they love to toil.

The whispers dance with every breeze,
They plot to steal the birds' sweet cheese.
While ants march by, they cause a fuss,
And all the while, the trees just blush.

Gnarled and wise, the roots proclaim,
"Oh, here we grow, it's quite a game!"
In their shade, the laughter swells,
As nature weaves its funny spells.

With every knot, they share a jest,
A playful twist, a humble quest.
In this comedy of life, they cheer,
Roots reveling in the fun they share.

Through the Eyes of the Young Oak

A young oak stands, so proud and tall,
Surveying all, it thinks it's small.
With limbs outstretched, it greets the sun,
"Hey there, buddy, let's have some fun!"

A curious leaf, it waves around,
"What's that over there? Is it playground ground?"
It spots a squirrel bouncing by,
"Can I join in? Oh my, oh my!"

With youthful dreams, it reaches wide,
Imagining adventures, far and side.
Each rustle brings a giggle, too,
In this world where wonders grew.

And while the forest shakes its head,
The oak declares, "I'll forge ahead!"
In laughter echoing through the trees,
A young dreamer dancing in the breeze.

Embracing the Sunlight

Hello, bright sun, come shine on me,
I'm ready to laugh, so let it be!
With each warm ray that tickles my bark,
I wiggle and giggle, it's quite the lark!

The daisies nod, they join the spree,
As butterflies flit, so wild and free.
"I swear I saw a shadow hop!"
They chuckle loud, not wanting to stop.

A cloud drifts by, with a frown so deep,
"I can't shine bright? I must not peep!"
But flowers whisper, "Join the delight,
For every shade makes laughter bright!"

Oh, to be kissed by this golden grace,
In the dance of life, we find our place.
With sunlight glowing, our spirits soar,
In nature's joy, we all explore.

Sprouts in Silent Soil

In a patch where whispers grow,
Tiny sprouts put on a show.
Hats made of leaf, they dance and sway,
In the mud, they laugh and play.

Worms are dancing down below,
Shouting, 'Hey, look at us go!'
The sun above sends down a beam,
Bringing warmth to this green dream.

A dandelion with golden fluff,
Says, "We may be small, but we're tough!"
They giggle as the wind comes near,
A gust arrives—oh dear, oh dear!

Then one sprout made quite a choice,
"Let's play pretend and use our voice!"
They sing to bugs in harmony,
Hoping one might join their spree.

Chronicles of a Young Oak

There once was a seed, oh so spry,
Declared, "I'll reach the sky!"
With roots that tickled the earth below,
It stretched out wide, steady but slow.

Squirrels passing often tease,
"Grow up quick and share your leaves!"
"Not yet!" he chuckled, swelling with pride,
"I've got to find my own groove inside."

A wise old stump once said, "Young tree,
Don't rush your height, be wild and free!"
So he wobbled and jiggled, grinned and bent,
Making tree friends that were heaven-sent.

With birdie banter overhead,
"Orbiting branches are my thread,"
The oak had plans for a mega nest,
Dreaming of being the very best.

Treetop Dreams

In a dreamland high above,
The trees hum tunes of peace and love.
Where branches twist in dizzy dance,
Leaves whisper secrets, take a chance.

A squirrel with shades and a skateboard,
Zooms past the branches, shouting, "I'm bored!"
The treetops chuckle, shake and reeled,
As he tumbles down, seeking a shield.

"Let's form a band!" the branches cried,
With drumsticks made of acorns, they tried.
Guitar strumming from the boughs so high,
Making melodies that touched the sky.

Frogs leap in for a serenade,
As the shadows dance, and fun cascades.
A festival of laughter takes flight,
In this woodland where joy ignites!

Journey of the Tender Shoot

Once a little sprout, in the breeze,
Wobbled and jiggled with such ease.
"Where do I go?" it pondered loud,
Beneath a sky slightly clouded.

A butterfly flew by, quite amazed,
"Your journey's cool, so be not phased!"
"Each drop of rain, each ray of sun,
Is part of a tale that's just begun."

So off it went, with roots dug deep,
Where silly bugs started to leap.
It startled a ladybug, oh dear!
Who shouted, "Nice shoes!" with a giggle and cheer.

With each new day, it grew in glee,
Finding friends beneath the tree.
And as the seasons came around,
It solidified its place in the ground.

Growing Beyond Shadows

In the garden, little sprout,
Wiggling roots, no room for doubt.
Chasing light with snappy flair,
While sneaky weeds just sit and stare.

Tiny leaves in a silly race,
They stretch and yawn, such a funny face.
The sunbeam giggles on their plight,
As they reach for it with all their might.

Dancing raindrops, such a sight,
A splashy party, what pure delight!
The worm in awe of their grand feat,
As they twirl and wiggle beneath his seat.

With each new inch, another cheer,
"Look at us now, we've grown, oh dear!"
But blushing blooms, they know the truth,
That growing up is really a hoot!

A Dance of Leaves

In autumn's breeze, the leaves go fly,
Doing twirls as they kiss the sky.
With laughter, they glide down to play,
Like clowns performing on a bright day.

Each one boasts shades of red and gold,
They giggle together, feeling bold.
'A swirl in the wind, let's shimmy again!'
While branches below shout, "Where've you been?"

The shivering boughs jealously sigh,
Watching leaves dance, oh my, oh my!
But roots whisper tales of earth's sweet embrace,
Knowing the leaves will find their place.

Then winter sneaks in with a frosty grin,
Leaves scatter away, oh where to begin?
"Don't fret!" they cry, "We'll be back real soon,
With summer's warmth, we'll dance to the moon!"

Chronicles of the Seedling

In the soil, a secret is found,
A sturdy seed, snug underground.
Dreaming of rays and raindrops to share,
Wishing for sunshine, not a care.

Up pops a sprout with a goofy grin,
"Hello, world! Where do I begin?"
With every wiggle, it shakes with glee,
"I'm the tallest tree for all to see!"

But shadows shout, "You're just a wee thing!"
And giggles erupt, like frogs in spring.
But our seedling laughs, "Watch me now soar!"
As it reaches for skies, forever more.

With the quirkiest moves, it spins and twirls,
In a festival of dirt, it blushes and curls.
"I'll grow so wise, and it won't be long,
I'll be the hero in nature's song!"

Braving the Storm

Beneath the clouds, a tiny leaf quakes,
As thunder rumbles, and lightning wakes.
With a puffed-up chest, it shouts, "I'm tough!"
While the wind just giggles, saying, "Not enough!"

The rain pours down like a wild slide,
Finding a puddle, the leaf takes a ride.
Spinning and splashing, a silly sight,
"Look at me go! I'm winning this fight!"

Then comes the sun with a warm embrace,
The leaf now beams, brightening the space.
"See, I survived that wild storm out there!
Now, who wants to join in my sun-kissed flair?"

But a raindrop giggles, "You're still quite small,
Just a splash in the game, but you gave it your all!"
"Ah, but I danced," the leaf proudly grinned,
As the clouds above started to rescind.

The Dance of the Tender Shoots

In the garden, shy sprouts sway,
Wiggling to the sun's bright ray.
With timid roots and leaves that twirl,
They have a groovy, leafy whirl!

Dancing round in joyful glee,
Branches jive as bugs agree.
Their little moves make all hearts cheer,
In this green world, there's nothing to fear!

Potting soil's their dance floor bright,
With worms as partners, oh what a sight!
Every drip from the watering can,
Is fuel for the plant party plan!

So let's celebrate this sprout parade,
Tiny dancers, not afraid.
With giggles and laughter, they will show,
Being small is where the fun will grow!

The Journey Towards Greatness

A little seed with dreams so vast,
Set out to grow, but it fell at last.
With one tiny root stuck in the muck,
It shouted, 'Hey, just give me some luck!'

Through puddles and pebbles, it waddled along,
Singing to clouds like a silly song.
Every tall tree had stories to share,
'You plant, you bloom, without a care!'

The wise old oak whispered, 'Do not rush,
Embrace your time, feel that gentle hush.'
So it danced in the breeze, gentle and light,
'I'll grow my way, and it'll be just right!'

With laughter and sun, it squeezed through the dirt,
Patience, it learned, is how dreams convert.
One day you'll rise, just wait and see,
Even a weakling can one day be free!

A Tapestry of Green

In the fields where greens collide,
A patchwork quilt, the critters confide.
Each blade of grass has a tale to weave,
With giggles and whispers, they all believe!

A clover claimed it's the luckiest sprout,
While dandelions danced and spun about.
Lively colors, a leafy display,
Nature's art show on a sunny day!

The daisies bobbed, and the thistles pranced,
With bees joining in, they all took a chance.
Each petal fluttered in a playful parade,
A riot of joy in the lush backyard glade!

So when you see this green tapestry,
Know it's woven with giggles and glee.
For in laughter and leaves, they all agree,
A garden of whims is the place to be!

Echoes of a New Canopy

As a sapling grows, it starts to sway,
Whispering secrets to leaves all day.
'Hey up there, I need some shade!'
Echoes of dreams in branches made.

With every gust, it starts to grin,
Hearing tales from trees worn thin.
Old trunks chuckle, sharing their lore,
'Hang in there, kid! There's so much more!'

The forest giggles, a symphony sweet,
Roots tap dancing beneath its feet.
From sun to rain, the notes will soar,
A concert of greenery forevermore!

So dance little sprout, let your voice ring,
Join in the chorus that nature will bring.
With laughter and light in every breeze,
You're part of this song, just think, if you please!

Sonnet of the Sapling

In a garden, a sprout took a leap,
It wobbled, it giggled, its roots went deep.
With sun on its face and a breeze for a friend,
It swayed with the joy that would never end.

The daisies chuckled, the bees sang a tune,
As the sapling danced under the watch of the moon.
"Don't grow too tall!" warned the gnome with a smile,
"Or we'll need a ladder to give you a guile!"

The Growth Chronicles

Once a tiny seed, oh so small,
Said to the earth, "I've plans for it all!"
"I'm not just a sprout, I'll take up some space,
And probably start a frisbee race!"

The squirrels rolled eyes, the birds stifled a laugh,
"Did you hear? He thinks he's got half the grass!"
But oh, he grew strong, with leaves full of cheer,
Challenging woodland friends to a game of 'who's here!'

The Awakening Grove

In the dawn of spring, the trees had a chat,
"Have you seen that sapling? He thinks he's all that!"
With leaves like a crown, he strutted about,
Convinced he was king, with no hint of doubt.

The acorns just rolled, laughing out loud,
"Look at him go, trying to stand proud!"
But when winds blew fierce, he bent to the ground,
"Okay, okay, I'm still small, but look at me rebound!"

Seeds of Change

In a patch of dirt, seeds plotted and schemed,
"What's our plan?" one brightly beamed.
"Let's hole up and wait till we're huge and tall,
Then we'll roll this garden, and have a ball!"

But just a few days, oh what a surprise,
A gopher came by with a gluttonous rise.
Suddenly their dreams of grandeur seemed tame,
As they waved goodbye in a greens-cheese game!

The Dance of Nature

In the meadow, plants do prance,
A daffodil in a silly dance.
The daisies twirl with all their might,
As butterflies join in pure delight.

The grass does giggle, soft and green,
While gophers peek, a playful scene.
A tree does sway, its branches tease,
Tickling the squirrel, oh what a breeze!

The wind joins in, it blows a tune,
Whistling loudly beneath the moon.
While daisies laugh and flowers cheer,
Nature's ball is drawing near!

So take a step, join in the fun,
In the dance of the day, with everyone.
A swirl of colors, a joyful show,
In this garden, smiles just grow!

Arise, Little Birch

Oh little birch, with bark so white,
You want to grow up, soar to new height.
But pesky bugs, they buzz and hum,
Your hat looks fine, but oh, that's gum!

You stretch your limbs towards the skies,
While critters shout their funny cries.
"Don't go too high!" a squirrel declares,
"Or you might fall and tangle your hairs!"

Yet onward you reach, with hopes so bold,
A teeny trunk that dreams of gold.
"I'll be a tree!" you bravely shout,
While ants parade and laugh about.

So rise up tall, embrace your fate,
With leafy dreams that resonate.
For every joke among your peers,
You'll grow grand too, despite your fears!

In the Shade of Potential

Under wide limbs where shadows play,
A little sprout dreams of the day.
"I'll be a giant!" it shouts with glee,
While worms below giggle, "You'll see!"

The sun pours down, oh, what a treat,
But watch out for ants on their speedy feet.
"Keep blossoming high!" the daisies cheer,
While butterflies wink, "We will be near!"

A breeze comes by, tickling leaves,
The tiny sprout laughs, "Who believes?"
For in this patch of curious fun,
Great stories start with just one run!

So if you see a sprout so bright,
Remember, laughter fills its flight.
In the shade of dreams where hopes ignite,
Potential's promise shines so light!

Sprig of Promise

In springtime's grip, a sprig appears,
Wiggling shyly, holding back fears.
"I'm just a twig!" it quips with pride,
As rabbits hop, "What's wrong with your ride?"

It dreams of leaves, of sunlit days,
Of dancing with the wind in playful ways.
"Just wait and see!" it calls with flair,
As busy bees buzz with a cheerful air.

But when the rain falls, it starts to pout,
"Oh no, what's this? Time to scream and shout!"
Yet gentle droplets play the game,
"Keep growing tall, to seek your fame!"

So sprig of promise, don't you fret,
You'll stretch out wide, and no regrets.
For in this garden, joy will bloom,
And soon you'll thrive, dispelling gloom!

Life's Young Amulet

In a pot sat a sprout, quite small,
Hoping to grow, to stand tall.
It dreamed of the sun, fair and bright,
But feared the cat, prowling at night.

With every day, it stretched and swayed,
Imagining victories, unafraid.
A leaf tickled a worm in its dance,
And together, they dreamt of a chance.

Beneath the soil, friends underground,
A party was held with laughs all around.
The radish told jokes, the beet sang sweet,
While beans made sure everyone had a seat.

So here's to the sprout, with a grin from leaf,
In the garden, it found its belief.
For every little laugh and cheer,
Brings joy to the garden year after year.

Leafy Legends

On a branch, a wise old tree,
Spoke of legends, wild and free.
"Once, I knew a flower so bright,
Who danced with bees, much to their delight."

The leaves leaned in, with ears so keen,
Hanging on tales they'd never seen.
"A snail once raced with a daring breeze,
Swapping stories beneath the trees."

An acorn piped up with a grin,
"I bet I'll be the first to win!"
But the tree just chuckled, shaking its bark,
"Just wait until you find the dark!"

So laughter echoed through branches wide,
As tales of mischief filled with pride.
In the forest of fun, they all agreed,
Life's a jolly race, as long as you lead!

The Gentle Surge

A tiny bud pushed through the ground,
With such excitement, it spun around.
"Watch out, I'm here!" it shouted with glee,
"I might be small, but I can be free!"

The wind blew softly, tickling the shoots,
While raindrops played the sweetest toots.
A dance took place in the morning sun,
As worms joined in, just having fun.

A ladybug cruised, wearing her spots,
"Let's race!" she called, tying up knots.
But the bud just laughed, feeling so bold,
"I'll grow to be big, just wait till I'm old!"

With giggles and whispers, they cheered it on,
In the garden, new friendships were born.
For in each gentle surge, life takes a leap,
In the laughter of leaves, secrets to keep.

A Symphony of Growth

In a garden where laughter bloomed,
Tiny seeds held a meeting, resumed.
"Let's grow to the sky, a grand tune to sing,
And turn this dirt into a sparkling bling!"

The daisies chimed in, full of glee,
"We'll twirl and swirl, just wait and see!"
While grasshoppers played their leafy lute,
And bumblebees added a buzzing flute.

Each sprout shared dreams of heights unknown,
Together they hummed, forming a throne.
A sunflower stood proud, with seeds in tow,
"I'll be the star of this garden show!"

As the sun set low in the brilliant sky,
The symphony played, oh my, oh my!
With every growl, giggle, and blow,
In the orchestra of blooms, fun would flow.

The Skyward Struggle

In a garden far and wide,
A tiny sprout felt filled with pride.
It stretched its leaves toward the sun,
But tangled up, oh what a run!

The butterflies, they made a fuss,
Dancing round like they were bus!
The little sprout just tried to sway,
And giggled as it lost its way!

A breeze came in with playful might,
Twisting branches left and right.
The sapling chuckled, 'What a ride!'
As it swayed like a silly tide!

With every flap and flutter near,
The sapling's giggles grew sincere.
In a tangle but fearlessly,
It laughed, "I'm still the best of me!"

Branches of Belief

In a forest filled with glee,
A branch declared, "Look here, it's me!"
It thought its wisdom needed share,
But other limbs just stood and stared.

"Embrace your leaves, it's all a game!
Don't fret about the wind's wild blame!"
The twigs around just shook their heads,
"Grow up, dear pain, and find the bed!"

With every word, it reached too high,
And bumped its bark against the sky.
"Oh, branches dear," it cried with zest,
"It's hard to lead, I'm feeling blessed!"

So they joined in, a branch brigade,
Creating laughter in the shade.
With wiggles, shakes, and silly shakes,
A celebration, no mistakes!

Dreams in Wooden Form

A little twig with grand designs,
Dreamt of being tall, like pines!
With every sunbeam, hope did bloom,
But half the time, it met with gloom.

"Why can't I reach the skies of blue?"
It pouted hard, "I'm wood, it's true!"
Yet every laughter from the birds,
Made dreams sprout out in silly herds.

It tried to sing with all its might,
But ended up just feeling slight.
"Oh, come on roots, let's give it flair,
And start a dance, have loads to share!"

With every twist and tiny sway,
The tree found joy—come what may!
In wooden form, its dreams unfurled,
A dance of whimsy, joy was swirled!

Thin Stems, Strong Souls

In the meadow, thin but bold,
Stems stood proudly, new and old.
"Who needs muscle? We are slick!"
They giggled loud, quick and quick!

"Watch us twist, watch us spin!
We're lighter than your little grin!"
They chirped and laughed, they twirled around,
Their laughter echoed through the ground.

One little leaf tried to show off,
But oh, it tripped, and started to scoff!
"I meant to show you all my flair!"
But petals landed here and there!

Yet every tumble turned to cheer,
"C'mon let's dance, the way is clear!"
Thin stems crossed paths, united free,
With strong hearts, they found their glee!

Newborn Forest

In the cradle of dirt, sprouted a sprout,
Wiggled and giggled, with no doubt.
Danced with the breeze, a leafy jig,
Whispered to sun, "Hey, look, I'm big!"

Tiny critters came, with curious eyes,
"What's the buzz? It's quite a surprise!"
A squirrel said, "Can you play charades?"
But the little seedling just rolled its fades!

Raindrops fell down, like jokes from the sky,
"Knock, knock!" they laughed, making the sprout spry.
"Who's there?" it replied, with a cheeky grin,
"Water! I'm here to help you begin!"

Day by day, roots tangled and twirled,
The sapling boogied; it was the best in the world!
The sun cheered, "Keep growing, dance more!"
And so, began the roots of folklore!

Resilient Roots

Watch those roots, they wiggle and twist,
Like funny little noodles, you can't resist!
Digging down deep, they play hide and seek,
Whispering secrets, oh so unique!

One cheeky root tickled a worm,
"Oh, stop it! You're causing a squirm!"
They wriggled and giggled, spread all around,
Making a party beneath the ground!

"Come join us!" called a pebble named Pat,
"A root rave's the best, wear your hat!"
So off they all danced, beneath the green,
With roots leading, it was quite the scene!

Through wind and rain, they jested and laughed,
Finding joy in the mess, love in the graft.
These roots had resilience, they'd grow and they'd bend,
For every odd twist, there's a new kind of trend!

Tender Echoes

In whispers soft, the leaves would talk,
Sharing old tales when the branches walk.
"Did you hear about the tree that could sneeze?"
It shook off its bark with the greatest of ease!

Echoes of laughter flew through the air,
As the breeze tickled branches with great care.
"Hey, listen close, there's a joke in the air!"
"A tree's best friend is the swing in despair!"

The twigs would chuckle, their giggles so bright,
While the trunks stood tall, like a sage in the night.
"Together we'll grow, through thick and through thin,
With each bounding laugh, let the fun begin!"

In the heart of the woods, joy would take flight,
Each tree in a tutu, a marvelous sight.
With echoes of fun, every day they unite,
In their whimsical world, laughter felt right!

Beyond the Bark

Beyond the bark, what wonders do lie?
A world filled with giggles under the sky.
"Hey tree, what's your favorite game?"
"Hide and seek! But I'm always the same!"

The branches waved, "What's your best prank?"
"Calling the squirrels, and filling their tank!"
"Oh dear," said a crow, "What a sticky mess!"
"Don't worry, old chap, it's all in jest!"

When shadows grew long, the creatures would gather,
"Life is a game, come join the banter!"
With roots intertwined, and laughter alight,
The forest was filled with delight!

So if you listen, beyond the bare bark,
You'll find a circus, a funny hallmark.
In every rustle, in every cheer,
Lies a silly secret, come lend me your ear!

A Tale of Sun and Soil

Once a seed with a dream, so bold,
Wished to grow into something of gold.
But with rain drops like marbles, it slipped,
Landed on a worm, and squealed, 'I'm equipped!'

A daisy laughed loud, with petals so bright,
'You're a sprout, not a plough, don't put up a fight!'
They trickled in sunbeams, while squirrels made bets,
On who'd spread the honey, and who'd get the nets!

Breath of the Tree

You see, a tree with a laugh, oh so grand,
Danced with the wind, at its leafy command.
'Take a deep breath!', it chuckled with glee,
'You'll be light-headed, just look at me!'

A squirrel yelled back, with a nut in its cheek,
'I'd breathe air if it weren't so bleak!'
They twirled and they pranced, through the branches,
they'd fly,
Chasing the clouds, oh my, oh my!

In the Embrace of Nature

In the woods where the critters all play hide and seek,
A sapling stood stiff, with legs weak and meek.
'Come join us!' chirped birds, 'We'll fluff up your leaves!'

But tripping on roots, it fell and grieved.

The flowers all giggled, with colors so bright,
'At least you don't have to wear socks, what a sight!'
As the sun warmed the ground, the sapling arose,
With a bow to the daisies, it bloomed with a pose.

Chronicles of a New Beginning

A tiny shoot whispered, 'Let's start a parade!'
With ants as the drummers, and shade as the grade.
But the grass danced so wildly, with roots all aglow,
They tripped on their tunes, fell flat on the flow.

The best plans,' laughed the breeze, 'are often quite silly!'

As butterflies jived, they forgot a bit frilly.
From acorns to oaks, they all took a turn,
In this woodland extravaganza, there's always a learn!

Birth of a Forest Hero

In a pot so snug, a sprout did sit,
Dreaming of heights and a leafy wit.
With sunlight's kiss and water's cheer,
He stretched up high, no hint of fear.

His roots dug deep, a clumsy dance,
He swayed to songs, took every chance.
The squirrels chuckled, the worms did gloat,
A hero born from just one little mote.

With each fresh breeze, he waved hello,
To passing bugs, a grand show-off, you know!
He wore a crown of acorns proud,
Making all the other plants feel quite cowed.

Now grown and wise, he claimed his throne,
With laughter echoing, he stood alone.
A forest hero, what a sight!
Sprouting giggles from morning to night.

The Awakening Grove

Once upon a time, in a grove so deep,
A sleepy old tree began to peep.
With a yawn and stretch, it shook off its dreams,
Woken by laughter, or so it seems.

A rabbit hopped in, with a skip and a leap,
Whispering jokes that made the roots weep.
The tree chuckled loud, branches shaking in glee,
Budding new leaves like a green confetti spree.

The blossoms blushed as the jokes took flight,
They giggled and snickered through day and night.
With every tickle of breeze on their face,
The grove became quite the funny place!

And so in the shade, the laughter did grow,
A joyful retreat where friends could just sow.
From shy little seeds to gregarious blooms,
They spread tales and giggles through all of their rooms.

A Twig's Triumph

From a tiny twig, a dream took flight,
To grow tall and strong – oh, what a sight!
With birdie friends chirping words of cheer,
He aimed for the sky, casting aside fear.

But twists and turns made him wobble and sway,
"Stand straight!" the leaves would yell and play.
With a shimmy and shake, he found his groove,
Becoming quite the branch that could really move!

The wind gave him hiccups, the rain made him dance,
Each wobble was just another chance.
He learned the rhythm of being a twig,
And soon cracked jokes, oh so big!

A twig's triumph was not just about height,
But the joy shared with friends, the pure delight.
In the end, he found his way to shine,
A little bit silly, and oh-so-divine!

Nature's Nurture

In the heart of the woods, what a sight to see,
Nature's nurturing hugs, wild and free.
From sunlit patches to puddled delight,
Every critter grinned in sheer delight.

The snails threw parties, the bugs played cards,
While owls read stories in their backyard yards.
Tree stumps as tables, with moss for a seat,
Laughter erupted—what a tasty treat!

Then came the winds, with their playful strife,
Making pinecones tumble, a merry old life.
Each leaf cheered on, with a swagger and spin,
Thick trunks wobbling, they'd all join in!

So gather your friends under nature's arms,
Let laughter abound; it's filled with charms.
For in every whisper, each rustle, each cheer,
Is a nature that loves us, always near!

Harmony in the Forest

In a forest filled with glee,
Trees dance like they're at a spree.
A squirrel juggles acorns bright,
While birds debate who's got the flight.

The mushrooms hold a little show,
In their hats, the rainbows glow.
They giggle at the falling leaves,
As the wind does playful heaves.

Bunnies hop to a merry beat,
Tails wagging to a tasty treat.
The owls hoot with a clever grin,
Joking that the night won't win.

So join this wacky woodland cheer,
For every critter's got a peer.
Together they laugh, they sing,
In this forest, joy's the king.

Awakening the Earth

Waking up in a fuzzy bed,
The worms stretch out, lightly fed.
A plant yawns and reaches high,
Saying 'Morning' to the sky!

The ants parade in perfect lines,
Counting crumbs like little mines.
The daisies whisper secrets dear,
As dew drops dance with chirp and cheer.

A beetle rolls a tiny ball,
While ladybugs just laugh and crawl.
The sun peeks in with a giggle bright,
Making shadows play in morning light.

So let the earth awaken grand,
Where mischief is a steady hand.
In every nook, a laugh is born,
To greet the day with joy reborn.

Silent Thriving

In the garden where the secrets lie,
The veggies plot their silent spy.
Tomatoes blush in the sun's warm gaze,
While carrots giggle in leafy maze.

Potatoes whisper tales of old,
Of burrowing deep, and growing bold.
The onions cry, but that's no foe,
It's just their way to steal the show.

Herbs shush each other in the breeze,
Sharing spicy secrets with absolute ease.
The cucumbers roll, a slippery race,
In this quiet world, they find their pace.

Though all seems calm, don't be misled,
For mischief stirs beneath the spread.
Silent thriving hides a laugh so sly,
Nature's antics quietly amplified!

Resilience of the Bud

A tiny bud peeks from the ground,
With dreams of growing all around.
It shakes off dirt with a snicker loud,
Saying, 'Watch me, I'll grow proud!'

The sun waves through the clouds above,
Gently coaxing with warmth and love.
With every raindrop, it starts to sway,
'Just wait and see,' it seems to say.

Neighbors bloom with colors bright,
Yet this bud holds its giggle tight.
It knows that patience is the key,
To burst forth wild, just wait and see!

So here's to buds, with smiles on their face,
In their timeless fight, they find their place.
Resilience shines in every small part,
For even buds can bloom with heart!

A Tender Stem's Tale

In a garden, green and bright,
A little stem claims its right.
It tries to stretch, but oh so slow,
Its pals just giggle, "Grow, friend, grow!"

A raindrop teases, falls with glee,
"I'm not a shower, just a pee!"
The stem, surprised, just shakes its head,
"I'll take my chances, I'll forge ahead!"

The sun beams down with cheeky flair,
"You think you'll sprout? Let's make a pair!"
But with each laugh, the stem stands tall,
"I'm here for laughs, just having a ball!"

A butterfly lands, a funny sight,
"Oh dear stem, you're quite the fright!"
They dance around in morning's glow,
"Together we'll put on a show!"

Forest Fables and Seedling Stories

Once in a forest, a seed did dream,
To be a tall tree, a mighty gleam.
But a squirrel laughed, with a nut in hand,
"You? A tree? Come on, that's grand!"

One day it sprouted, so proud and spry,
But a gust of wind made it sigh.
"I'm not ready! Oh, please don't blow!"
While the breezes danced, putting on a show.

Then came a robin, with jokes to tell,
"You've got the style, you're doing so well!"
They chirped and giggled beneath the leaves,
"Just wait, my friend, you'll soon achieve!"

The sapling stiffened, braving the jest,
"I might be small, but I'll be the best!"
And roots dug deeper, with each hearty laugh,
"Let's find more fun on this leafy path!"

Whispered Winds of Growth

A tiny bud in the sun did lie,
With dreams of reaching for the sky.
A breeze blew past, a playful tease,
"Don't get too cozy, it's not a breeze!"

The earthworms chuckled, wiggling near,
"You think you'll bloom? Oh, have no fear!"
A robin shouted, summoning cheer,
"Your time will come, just persevere!"

As clouds rolled in, a drizzle came,
"Oh no! I'm drowning! Who's to blame?"
But with each drop, the stem stood stout,
"Just watering the roots, that's what it's about!"

In moonlit nights, they shared more quips,
The sprout's tall tales, and leaf-spun trips.
With every laugh, it grew more bright,
A tiny hero, in nature's light!

Garden of Possibilities

In a garden full of colorful dreams,
A little bud waved, bursting at the seams.
"I'm gonna be a sunflower tall!"
But daisies whispered, "You're still so small!"

With every worm that crawled nearby,
It giggled, "Hey, let's reach for the sky!"
A playful breeze made petals dance,
"Why wait for summer? Let's take a chance!"

The sunflower blushed, feeling quite brave,
"I'll show you all how to misbehave!"
With roots that wiggled, reaching deep,
"I'm here for the laughter, not just to peep!"

And when the moon above did peek,
The garden laughed, oh so unique!
Each sprout a story, a whimsical tale,
Creating a chorus that would never pale!

Celestial Canopies

Beneath the stars, a tiny sprout,
Said, "I'm a tree!" with a giggle and pout.
The moon just chuckled, the sun rolled its eyes,
"You'll need some years before the surprise."

With dreams of shade, it danced in the breeze,
But ants held a meeting, a plan to tease.
"Let's paint its trunk with gooey old gum,
So all passing squirrels will go, 'What a bum!'"

As clouds passed overhead, it shouted aloud,
"Why can't I grow taller, I'm feeling too proud!"
A bird laughed and said, "Just be patient, dear friend,
Your chapter is starting, but it's not the end."

So there it stood, with a grin on its face,
Making friends with the critters all over the place.
In this patch of green, it finally found,
That laughter and friendship were always around.

The Genesis of Growth

Once a seed in the dirt thought it would bloom,
"Just wait till I'm tall, I'll clear out this room!"
But the worms all just laughed, "That's quite the goal!
You're just a small snack for a digging mole!"

Every day it would stretch, reaching for the sky,
The grasshoppers cheered, "Oh my, oh my!"
But the passing butterflies would tease and would jest,
"Just wait till your leaves are put to the test!"

And yet with each droplet of rain upon ground,
The sprout wiggled fiercely, its joy knew no bound.
"Why be just a sprout, when I could be grand?
With limbs like a giant, and roots like a band!"

So a promise it made, to reach for the light,
And outsmart the critters that scurried at night.
With humor and hope, it continued to grow,
In this journey of green, it discovered the show!

Flora's First Steps

In the garden quite green, a flower did sprout,
With petals all floppy, it wobbled about.
"I'm here for the sunshine, no time for a frown!
Just watch me dazzle in my floral gown!"

The bees all buzzed with a grin and a flare,
"Look at her dancing, swaying without care!"
But the bugs whispered softly, in a fluttery way,
"She thinks she's a queen, but who will she sway?"

Yet each sunny morning, with dew on her face,
Florals laughed soft as they joined in the race.
"I'll grow all my colors!" she proudly declared,
The tulips all nodded, like they really cared!

Then a breeze came through, with giggles to share,
And Flora twirled round, with her flair in the air.
"I'm not just a flower, I'm a party, you see!
So bring all the critters, and let's have a spree!"

A Sylvan Symphony

In a forest of friends, where the laughter was loud,
A tiny green sprout wanted to make its crowd.
"Gather 'round, critters! Come hear my great song!
I'm destined for greatness; this won't take long!"

The deer rolled their eyes, while the rabbits all giggled,
While squirrels just muttered, "This sprout must be tickled!"
But the sprout stood its ground, a tune in its heart,
"Just wait till I flourish, then I'll be a part!"

A raccoon with style wore a hat made of leaves,
"Yes, you can sing, but can you weave sleeves?"
The sprout, with a grin, said, "I might need some class,
But I'll grow to be fab, just give me some sass!"

As the sun set low, and the stars shone so bright,
The forest joined in, oh, what a delight!
In a symphony sweet, every voice became free,
"Who knew a small sprout could create such a spree?"

Shadows of the Growing Tree

A little tree had a dream,
To tower tall and be supreme.
But goats nearby thought it was grand,
To munch those leaves like they were planned.

With every chew, the tree would sway,
"Hey, leave my branches, if you may!"
But goats just bleated, full of glee,
While shadows chuckled, full of spree.

The sun would shine, then clouds would roam,
This sapling smiled, still far from home.
It danced and twisted with pure joy,
While squirrels tried to steal its toy.

The shadows cast a playful game,
As tiny critters joined the fame.
Each gust of wind would send them flying,
The little tree, it kept on trying.

Petals of Perseverance

A flower bloomed amidst the weeds,
With petals bright, it sparked some needs.
It laughed aloud in colorful hues,
Despite the bugs who drank its blues.

It told the bees, "Please come and play!"
But they just buzzed and flew away.
"Why can't you sit and have a sip?"
As pollen fell, it did a flip.

With every rain, it sang so loud,
A melody that drew a crowd.
The ants all danced, though tiny they were,
Moving as if in a grand ballet blur.

Yet still the weeds grew tall and rough,
"I'll sprout through you, it's just a bluff!"
With a wink and a twist, it claimed its throne,
A little hero among the grown.

Hope in Every Leaf

A leaf once dreamed of soaring high,
To catch the winds and touch the sky.
It flapped around, but then got stuck,
   On the nose of a passing duck.

"Oh, feathery friend, I take a ride!"
The duck just quacked, albeit wide-eyed.
With every waddle, the leaf would cheer,
"We'll conquer skies, let's go my dear!"

They soared above the fields of green,
   Where mischief lurked, or so it seemed.
Through gusts of laughter, they would glide,
   While ducklings trailed, unable to hide.

And when they fell, the world turned round,
   The leaf just giggled, "What a sound!"
     Into the puddle, it took a dive,
   Where tiny frogs sang, "We're alive!"

Roots that Reach

Beneath the soil, the roots had dreams,
To stretch and wiggle, or so it seems.
They whispered through the earth so deep,
While worms would giggle and then repeat.

"Let's reach for water, let's find some fun!"
The roots all cheered, 'We've got this one!'
Yet every stone just laughed and teased,
"You'll never move, you're so uneased!"

But roots, determined, dug and sprawled,
Through rocky tunnels, they crawled and crawled.
They tickled legs of moles that scurry,
With every twist, they'd laugh in a hurry.

At last, they found a stream so bright,
With joyful splashes, they danced in light.
From deep below, they sang their song,
"Together we are where we belong!"

Whispers of Young Roots

In a garden not so grand,
A sprout wobbled, took a stand.
It called out to the worms with glee,
"Let's dance today, come jive with me!"

The ladybug flew by with flair,
"Who knew you could grow without a care?"
The roots just giggled underground,
As nature's fun was all around.

With sunlight streaming, giggles' charm,
The tiny buds were quite the swarm.
"Hats off, dear beetles, it's a rave,
And we're the sprouts that you must save!"

The daisies sighed, "Oh what a sight,
Let's throw a party, it feels so right."
So here they grew, those seedlings spry,
Not just plants, but stars on high!

Dawn of the Tender Sprout

In the morning light so bright,
A sprout peeked out with sheer delight.
With dew drops twinkling, oh what fun,
It planned its day under the sun.

"Hey, Mr. Squirrel, come have a snack,
I've got some leaves, no need to pack!"
But the squirrel, clever and spry,
Just stole a leaf and said, "Oh my!"

The robin chirped, "You're all too green,
But oh, the joy that I have seen!
Each little leaf, a stage, a chance,
Let's all partake in this fine dance!"

And so they twirled in morning rays,
While roots below held secret ways.
With laughter echoing through the glade,
A party started, swiftly laid!

Journey of the Green Dream

A little seed embarked one day,
On a journey, bold and bray.
"I'll find adventures, sights so grand,
Just wait and see, I'll take a stand!"

Through muddy puddles, a slip and slide,
A tiny worm said, "Come, let's ride!"
They rolled and tumbled, what a sight,
"Who knew plants could take flight?"

With every petal opened wide,
Each new friend was full of pride.
"Let's climb the sky!" the sunflower cried,
But the wind just chuckled, "Try and glide!"

And as the sunset painted hues,
The little seed learned lots of views.
The world was big, yet close and neat,
With every inch, a funny treat!

Echoes in the Canopy

Up high among the leaves so green,
The tallest tree, a sight unseen.
"Oh dear," it sighed, "I can't recall,
Did I forget my roots at all?"

The branches swayed, a gentle tease,
"Maybe try a stretch or sneeze!"
Suddenly, a bird flew by,
"Just sing a note, and then you'll fly!"

The chirps of joy cascaded down,
As silly shadows danced around.
Each leaf began to sway and laugh,
"Who knew we'd find a magic path?"

So echoes rang from trunk to bough,
"Here's to friendship, we'll make a vow!"
With playful hearts in a leafy spree,
The canopy sang—"Be bold, be free!"

Through the Seasons of Change

In springtime sun, a sprout did peek,
Wiggly worms had quite the cheek.
They danced around, they spun and twirled,
While seedlings giggled, oh what a world!

Summer arrived with a blast of heat,
The little leaves dashed for shade, quite neat.
Sunbathers, they whispered, 'We're growing tall!'
But bugs in bikinis ate them, the gall!

Then autumn came, with colors bold,
The saplings shivered, feeling quite old.
They dressed in gold, red, and all that jazz,
While squirrels sang, 'We're all such a class!'

Winter's chill brought blankets of white,
The young trees wished for the sun's warm light.
They stamped their roots in the frosty ground,
And dreamed of springtime when joy would abound.

The First Raindrop

A tiny leaf felt a drop in the sky,
She looked all around, gave a little sigh.
'It's just a tease!' shouted her friend,
'Wait til we're soaked, then we'll ascend!'

Then plop! A puddle formed with a splash,
The roots started dancing; oh, what a bash!
'Let's swim and twirl,' shouted the stalks,
As nearby frogs croaked their funny talks.

With each new drop, they laughed out loud,
Inviting the wind to join in the crowd.
'We are the rulers of this little pond!'
Just then a duck waddled, chirped, and yawned.

But when the clouds darkened with a frown,
The little twig roared, 'Don't let us drown!'
They bobbed and weaved in the rain's delight,
'This is the party, it's quite out of sight!'

A Twig's Voyage

A twig set sail on a leaf-shaped boat,
On a breezy day, he began to float.
With a push from the wind, he waved goodbye,
'Here's to the ocean, oh my oh my!'

The raindrops splashed, 'Are we in a lake?'
The twig giggled, 'No, but make no mistake!'
His buddies laughed, 'We'll all float along,
'Til we find land and sing our own song!'

They caught a wave, tumbled round and round,
The plankton danced, while seagulls swarmed the sound.
'Next stop, the shore!' the twig called with glee,
But the wind laughed, 'You're staying with me!'

Finally ashore, they landed with zest,
And all the critters came for the fest.
'Life's quite a trip!' cheered the brave little twig,
'Next time let's try with a much bigger gig!'

The Quiet Awakening

In the stillness of dawn, a bud did yawn,
Stretching its leaves as the night was gone.
'What a slept-in day!' it declared with a cheer,
While nearby ants whispered, 'We're glad you're here!'

Butterflies flitted, painting the sky,
The bud grinned wide, letting out a sigh.
They played peek-a-boo with the sun's warm glow,
'This is the fun, just watch us grow!'

Then came the breeze with a playful nudge,
The little bud giggled, 'Oh please, don't judge!'
For when you're a sprout in the light of the morn,
Every day is a chance to be reborn.

And so, as new blooms kissed the skies,
The world turned bright before their eyes.
With laughter of leaves and joy in the air,
They danced through the garden, without a care.

The Unfolding Journey

In a pot on the sill, it stood quite still,
Dreaming of forests, where it could fulfill.
With nary a breeze, it swayed with glee,
Yet tripping on roots was a sight to see!

One sunny day, a seedling peeked,
'Hello, dear sapling!' it lightly squeaked.
The pot gave a creak, the soil did shake,
'Uh-oh, I'm dreaming, or will I break?'

With little green leaves, it dashed to the sun,
Saying, 'Watch out world, I'm ready for fun!'
A dance with the wind, a jig with the rain,
One twirl too many, oh what a strain!

But laughter erupted as a breeze came by,
Tickling the leaves and making them sigh.
'I may trip and tumble, but I'm still here!
Each flip in the air fills me with cheer!'

Aroma of Earth's Embrace

In the garden of giggles, where tomatoes grow,
A small sprout awoke, 'Well, here we go!'
It sniffed at the dirt, 'Mmm, what a scent!'
Playing hide and seek, it was heaven sent.

A worm gave a wink, slithering by,
Said, 'You'll need more than leaves to reach the sky!'
The sprout puffed out its chest, looking quite bold,
'I'll have you know, I'm a sight to behold!'

With roots looking fancy and leaves so bright,
It danced with the daisies till late at night.
'Come join in the fun!' it giggled in glee,
A cacophony of laughter, as wild as can be!

But in all the frolic, a raindrop came down,
Splashing fun everywhere, oh how it drowned!
Squeezed between puddles, joy turned to fright,
'Oops! Soggy's not stylish, but isn't it light?'

Lullabies of the Understory

Beneath a bigger tree, the young sprout would hum,
Singing sweet tunes that made the critters come.
'Hey there, little critters, don't be so shy,
Join my sing-along, let's reach for the sky!'

A squirrel sat perched, with a nut in hand,
'You're quite ambitious for a tree so bland!'
But the sprout just giggled, 'With roots this wide,
I'll be a legend, with branches to ride!'

A hedgehog chimed in, 'You're quite the dreamer!'
'Dreaming is my job,' came the sprout's beamer.
'Watch me, dear friends, I'll grow up just right,
And throw the best parties every moonlight!'

So nights filled with laughter, and days filled with cheer,
The sprout learned to revel, with friends always near.
One whisper in the wind, 'Let's dance through the leaves!'
And soon a great party, no one would believe!

The Little Tree That Could

Once a tiny sapling with dreams oh so vast,
'Watch out! I'm coming; I'll grow up fast!'
With every small wiggle and wobbly sway,
It practiced its stance for the grand tree ballet.

A butterfly giggled, 'You think you can dance?'
The sapling replied, 'Give me just one chance!'
With every new leaf, it twirled and it spun,
Showing each garden that it's here for fun!

The fence-watching flowers began to cheer loud,
'This little tree's courage is making us proud!'
It giggled and shimmied, feeling quite grand,
While the critters all clapped, lending a hand.

And as seasons passed, it grew tall and wide,
But deep in its heart, would be laughter inside.
For the tree knew well, as it danced through the day,
A little bit of joy goes a long, long way!

Nature's Young Prodigy

In the garden, where flowers chat,
A little sprout wore a funny hat.
It danced in the breeze, all green and spry,
Whispering jokes to the buzzing fly.

They laughed and twirled in the sun's warm glow,
While ants marched by in a neat little row.
"Why did the tree make a fancy show?"
"To impress the roots down below!"

But oh how the sun would tease and play,
"Is that your best fit for a sunny day?"
The sapling grinned and gave a twirl,
"I'm the freshest thing in this floral world!"

So let the petals join the fun,
With laughter shared under the sky so fun.
Our hero here, with leaves so bright,
Is the life of the party, what a sight!

Flourishing in the Shadow

In a forest filled with towering dreams,
A cheeky sapling plotted silly schemes.
"Why stand in sunlight when I can hide?"
"I'm thriving in shadows, come take a ride!"

Mossy friends giggled with bouncy glee,
"We're the coolest club—just you wait and see!"
Whispering secrets, they plotted their fun,
In the cool dampness, they'd laugh 'til they're done.

"I can't grow tall, but I'm hip and I'm wise,
With my playful shade, I'll win this prize!"
A squirrel peeked in with a scruffy old grin,
"You're bringing the fun, let the antics begin!"

With laughter echoing, under boughs so grand,
The shadows transformed, nature's own band.
No sunbeam needed for this playful spree,
In shady delight, we're totally free!

Together they flourished, a quirky brigade,
Making their shade a quirky crusade.
So here's to the saplings in darkness bright,
Finding their joy in the absence of light!

Embracing the Light

A little shoot stretched its limbs so wide,
Seeking the sun with joy and pride.
"Catch me if you can!" it called to the shade,
While butterflies giggled and twirled in parade.

"Don't be shy, join my radiant dance,"
Said the sprout with a mischievous glance.
Light tickled the leaves like a zealous friend,
As roots grumbled, "Oh, will this ever end?"

A jolly old worm wiggled deeply below,
"You're reaching too high, taking a show!"
But the sapling just laughed, with a twirling sway,
"I'm a superstar in the garden today!"

So it basked in the rays, so proud and spry,
While shadows beneath would sigh and try.
But bright little sprout didn't mind any blight,
For embracing the light was its pure delight!

A Sapling's Heartbeat

In a garden where magic comes alive,
A sapling danced with its pulse to thrive.
"Thump, thump, thunk! Can you hear my beat?"
It rhymed with the raindrops, oh, what a treat!

"Roots going deep, as I sway and prance,
I'm tap dancing happily, what a chance!"
The flowers all giggled, in colors so bold,
"Who knew that the sapling had moves to uphold?"

Sunshine above gave the rhythm a glow,
While clouds played DJ, with beats down below.
Bees joined in, with their buzzing delight,
Creating a concert beneath the starlight.

So here's to the sapling, with heart full of glee,
Finding its rhythm, living wild and free.
With each little wiggle, it sings through the day,
In a world full of laughter, come dance, come play!

www.ingramcontent.com/pod-product-compliance
Lightning Source LLC
Chambersburg PA
CBHW071822160426
43209CB00003B/175